ITCHES INSIDE MY HEAD

VOLUME I

RANDY MAZIE

Itches Inside My Head
Randy Mazie
ISBN 979-8-9850209-4-6 (Paperback)
ISBN 9798801388809 (Amazon Hardcover)

Published by
A Year of Encouragements Press, LLC
www.ayearofencouragements.com
mail@ayearofencouragements.com

Please visit our website for more information about this and other books, order links,
forums, and contact information.

Front cover by Luke Valentine.
Dedication page by Garrett Madlock.
All poem illustrations by Luke Valentine
(with exception of the opening page, pages 42/43, bottom of page 61, and the Index).
Back cover by Garrett Madlock.
Interior design and typesetting by Heather Slawecki, graylynpress.com.

This is dedicated to you.

Because you like to laugh and play.　　Because you

giggle

when you

hiccup.

Because you can see the world　　　upside down.

Be

ca

us

e

your nose is run

n

y.

Be　　　　　　　　　　　　　　is.

ca　　　　　　　　　　　　　　th

use　　　　　　　　　read

you're　　　　as you

SMILING

And to my grandchildren:

Tyler, Gauge, Brooklyn,

and the one who's coming soon!

WOW, THAT WAS FUN.

NOW, WHERE'S THE FIRST PAGE?

A CHILD ONLY A MOTHER COULD LOVE

My feet are too big.
My hair's a bad wig
and my nose is pushed off to one side.
My ears are like wings.
My mouth says such things
that embarrass me deep down inside.

But never-the-less,
in spite of the mess
that I am and I always will be,
my mother says this,
as she plants a kiss
on my cheek, she will always love me!

HOW TO BUILD A BIRDHOUSE

Get some wood.
Get a saw.
Cut in half.
Cut some more.
Get a hammer.
Get some glue.
Get some nails
and a screw.
Get a Band-Aid.
Dig a hole.
Strap the birdhouse
on a pole.
Sit back very
satisfied.

But wait!

We nailed
the cat inside.

3

DAD AND I WATCH SUNDAY FOOTBALL

As dad sat down, he said his bones ache.
I said, "Mine do too."
He said, "That's 'cause you're growing up."
I said, "You are too."
He said he doubted that was true.

"I'm only growing 'round my waist,"
my father said to me.
"And nothing's growing on my head."
He bent so I could see.
I said none of that meant much to me.

"Thank you, son," my father said,
"I love you too."
He smiled and settled in his chair.
I sat in my chair too.
And there we were just doing what
two grown men love to do.

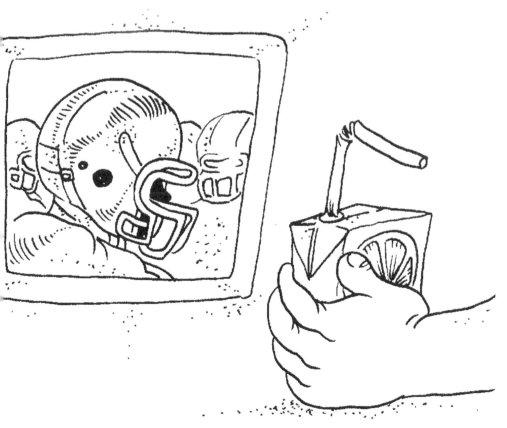

LOVEABLE LILLY

Loveable Lilly loves red lollipops.
Once she starts licking them
      she never stops.
Licking and licking them
      down to the stick,
then licking the paper
      and crying out, "Yick!"

Loveable Lilly bought pops by the cases.
She'd challenge her friends
    to lollipop races.
Who could lick 'em the quickest
    and lick 'em the most?
But she'd always win.
    "I'm the best!" she would boast.

Funny thing happened as the years went along.
Lillian's tongue
    got longer than long.
It first grew by inches,
    and then grew by feet,
until it stretched down from her mouth
    to the street.

Lilly now lives on a green lily pad.
We call her "The Frog,"
    which gets her so mad.
But she now catches flies
    with a flick of her tongue
and still licks her lollipops
    after each one.

OOPS!

I brought an elephant
inside a restaurant.

I asked if he would dine
with my friend porcupine.

He was so delighted
that he was invited.

We told the Maitre D'
to set a place for three.

But nowhere could he sit
because he could not fit.

To save us from embarrassment,
the Maitre D', with good intent,
said without a moment's hesitation,

"Sorry, but you have no reservation..."

HOME
SWEET
HOME

THE INSIDE OUT INN AT OUTSVILLE

I stayed at an Inn in Outsville.
Its name was Inside Out.
Which meant each time that I walked in
that I was walking out.

When people said to me, "Look out!"
they really meant, "Look in!"
which I could never figure out
'cause I couldn't figure in.

There were other Inns in Outsville,
but they were further out,
which wasn't very far away,
'cause in was further out.

There were fast food restaurants,
with windows called "Drive-out."
You drove your car inside the store
and took the "take-in" out.

And when I left the Inn, they said,
"You better not go out."
"I know," I said, " 'Cause if I'm in,
I never will get out."

So, in I went and out I came,
and left the "Inside Out."
I'll never know if I was in
'cause I never did get out.

COUSIN SKYLAR'S GOT THE BIGGEST BITE!

Cousin Skylar's got the biggest bite!
It's huge and red and sore.
He didn't see what bit him,
but he's rolling on the floor.

Come quick. You got to help him!
He's crying quite a lot.
He's yelling for Aunt Laurie.
He says his head is hot.

I told him, Take it easy.
I said, I'll be right back.
He cried, Hurry, and he grabbed my shirt.
Then I gave him quite a whack.

It wasn't right, yes, I admit.
I kind of whacked him twice.
Then he kicked me *really* hard—
it wasn't very nice.

He screamed and yelled and hollered.
He said I was a "jerk."
Well, that was it—something snapped!
And then I *really* went berserk.

He might be crying from the bite,
or when I knocked him to the ground.
But you got to come real quick!
He's flopping all around.

GWEN THE HEN

Gwen the Hen,
    now and then
wanted to be different.
For who she was
    and what she does
was sometimes insufficient.
She'd cluck away,
    buck-buck all day
which left her discontent.
Each day the same.
    Oh, who could blame
her grand experiment!

She put a nose ring in her beak,
a red tattoo upon her cheek,
dyed all her feathers deep dark blue,
she wouldn't cluck, she'd only coo.
She swears she'll never lay more eggs.
She wears black tights around her legs.
When she struts by, the roosters crow,
and Gwen the Hen gives them a show.

She's happy now as she can be.
She's quite a little chick-a-dee.

19

GERTIE McDOUGLE

Gertie McDougle
would play the bugle,
but all of her notes would be sour.

We'd yell, "Gertie, stop!"
We'd wave and we'd hop,
but on she would play for an hour.

THERE'S A GIANT SLEEPING UNDER MY BED

There's a giant sleeping under my bed.
I can tell by the way that I'm feeling.
There's a giant sleeping under my bed.
I sat up and my head hit the ceiling!

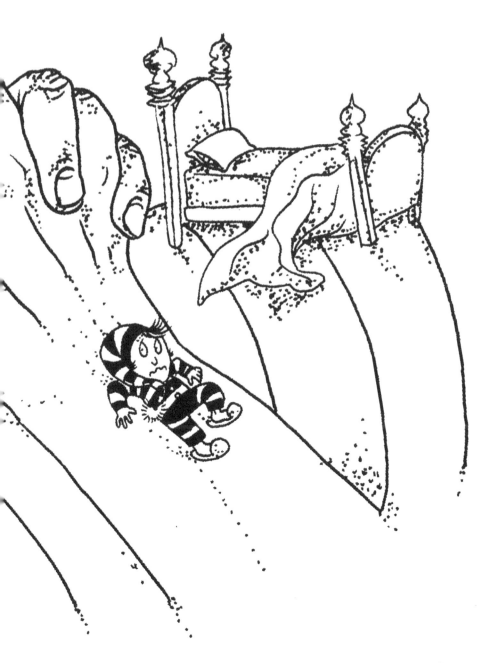

I AM MY DAD'S MECHANIC

My dad and I, we fix cars.
We put them up on jacks.
We raise them high up in the sky,
so we won't break our backs.

We wear our hats and overalls.
We use our socket wrenches.
We change the wheels and stop the squeals
as we sit upon our benches.

We change the filter and the oil.
We flush the radiator.
All is good, under the hood,
when we clean the carburetor.

Dad takes a break, but I still work.
I fix the axle stubble.
The seismic motor and the rotor
were giving me some trouble.

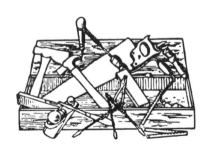

I changed the pulleys and the belts
that inhibit the injector.
I put them back, so there's no slack.
Then dad is the inspector.

He says it is a job well done.
He says I'm his mechanic.
But when he sees just what I've done,
I think he starts to panic.

OH!

While we were climbing up a hill,
"Let's play a game," said Joe.
"After everything I say,
You have to shout out—'Oh!'"

"I listen to the radi..."—"Oh!"
"I like playing tic-tac-t..."—"Oh!"
"My best friend is Anthoni..."—"Oh!"
"He lives in New Mexic..."—"Oh!"
"Honey's made in Tupel..."—"Oh!"
"We'll shuffle off to Buffal..."—"Oh!"

Then Joe said, "You need to kn..."—"Oh!"
"I suffer bad from vertig..."—"Oh!"

"Too late! Watch out bel..."—"Oh!
                    Oh!
                    Oh!"

ITCHES INSIDE MY HEAD #1

I had an itch inside my head.
I knew not what to do.
Until I smelled some pepper,
and I scratched it with "Achoo!"

NOTHING IS REALLY THAT STRANGE

Birds that swim,
        fish that fly,
I sit by my window
        and watch them go by.

Books that read to you,
        dogs walking cats,
Halloween witches play
        baseball with bats.

Zoos with caged people,
        a lollipop sea,
phones that groan
        and cry, "Answer me!"

Purple bananas,
        a clock with a face,
hundreds of snails
        lined up for a race.

A horse who lays eggs
        and nests in a tree,
these are the things
        that are going past me.

It takes getting used to
        seeing things change,
but nothing, oh nothing,
        is really that strange…

I HAD A HORRIBLE NIGHTMARE LAST NIGHT

I was a cricket who got into a fight
with a terrible toad,
  a frivolous frog,
who then picked a fight
  with a pompous hedgehog,
who was churlish and scrappy
  and snapped at a goat,
who was stubborn, unyielding,
  and went for his throat,
but slipped in the mud,
  head-butted a hog,

who hit him quite hard
        on his head with a log.
As they bleated and squealed,
        the farmer ran out,
with pitchfork in hand,
        I heard him shout,
which frightened the mule,
        who started to bray,
kicking the farmer,
        who flew in the hay,
and quickly, so quickly,
        we all ran away.

IF...

If blue was red
and red was blue,
could you choose
        between the two?

If night was day
and day was night,
could you sleep
        with all that light?

If play was school
and school was play,
would you go
        to school each day?

If peas were cookies
and cookies were peas,
would you ask,
        "More peas, please?"

If things stayed the same
and you were to change,
would the usual things
        begin to feel strange?

35

THE MORNING BIRDS

Caw. Caw. Tweet.
Caw. Caw. Tweet.
Chirp. Chirp. Chirp.

In words we do not understand
the morning birds:
Chitchat. Chitchat.

Caw. Caw. Tweet.
Caw. Caw. Tweet.
Chirp. Chirp. Chirp.

37

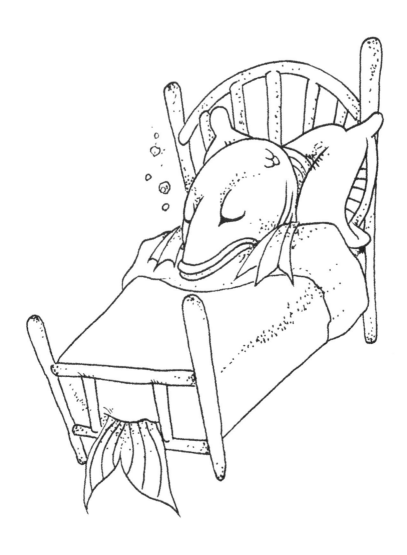

FISH (haiku)

When it rains do fish
still swim? Or do they hurry
home to nice warm beds?

BUSYBODY BUMBLEBEE

The buzzing bumblebee
buzzed busily by me.
Busybody bumblebee
stopped to take a look at me.

Busybody!

I TOLD A LIE

It was the best lie
        I have ever told.
It was big and bold—
        it just came out.
I didn't even try to think it through.
It sounded true. And there was nothing
        mom or dad could say or do.

They were shocked.
        So was I.
I didn't even blink
        or bat an eye.
I didn't even try to hold my breath,
though the words I said had
        scared me half to death.

I told a lie.

It was the best lie
        I have ever said.
I didn't even sweat
        or turn bright red.
I pulled it off.
I didn't stutter
        or begin to cough.

What's that you ask?
        What did I say?
Well, I looked them straight
        into their eyes
and said, "I'm sorry. I apologize."
And they believed me.
        I swear it's true.

Sometime you should try it too!

ANSWER THESE QUESTIONS

Answer these questions.
     Answer them fast.

If I am first,
     will I ever be last?
If I am quick,
     will I ever be slow?

If I say yes,
       will the answer be no?
If I try hard,
       will I always succeed?

Answer these questions.
       Answer them, please.

SHELBY AND AMOUR

Shelby got a cat, cat, cat.
She named the cat "Amour."
She loved the cat—so much that
she went and got five more.

Then five more and then five more,
more and more and more and more!
(Shelby had this cat rapport.)

We don't see Shelby anymore,
only cats—from door to door.
Kitty litter in a mound.
Fuzzy fur floats all around.
Paws and claws on all the floors.
Meows that sound—like lions' roars!

Sneezing, wheezing—as we walk by,
we only see big hairballs fly,
never Shelby or "Amour."
(They're lost amidst the cat décor.)

MINI MENAGERIE MERRY-GO-ROUND

I had a dog
     who licked my cat
every time she purred.

And my cat purred
     each time she heard
the chirping of my bird.

My bird would chirp
     and chirp and chirp
each time my dog would lick

my cat who purred
     each time she heard
the chirping of my bird.

I would yell and holler
     but it wouldn't do the trick.
Every time I'd scream, STOP!
     my dog would start to lick,
my cat would purr,
     my bird would chirp,

     I'm getting very sick!

Anybody want a pet?

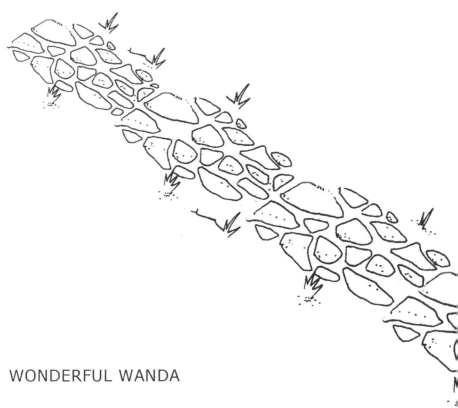

WONDERFUL WANDA

Wonderful Wanda would wander wherever
and wondered and pondered if ever there ever
were others who wandered wherever and wondered
and pondered if ever there ever was Wanda.

THE THRILL...

of fishing is catching the fish.
of seeing the first star is making the wish.
of the ending of school is the starting of play.
of getting the test back is getting an "A."

of tying shoelaces is getting it right.
of windy days is flying a kite.
of playing baseball is winning the game.
of making a campfire is watching the flame.

of reading a poem is learning new things.
of playing checkers is getting kings.
of wearing a hat is having a head.
of feeling exhausted is going to bed.

ITCHES INSIDE MY HEAD #2

"I have an itch inside my head."
"You must mean OUT," my good friend said.
"No, I mean in. I don't mean out."
He stared at me. I felt his doubt.
And so, my head he did inspect.
To find out why "in" was correct.
And when he saw his knowledge lacked,
he cried...

"Of course, it's in. Your head is cracked!"

TATTOO!

Tattoo my chest, arms, and face.
Tattoo every single space.
Tattoo everywhere you can—
Then call me, "The Tattoo Man."

THE BEASTIE BOY

A new boy started class one day
and asked me if I'd care to play.
I must admit that he was strange
for while we played, I watched him change.

Where once were ears on this boy's head,
were now antennae there instead.
His mouth had vanished from his face.
I gulped! Two fangs were in its place!

He'd grown six legs and round green eyes.
This beast had grown to twice my size.
I screamed and ran. It buzzed and flew.
It shrieked, "*I'm coming to get you!*"

It swooped down fast, took me away
and no one's seen me 'til today.
What's that? You doubt my story's true?
You think that I have lied to you?

I'm new in class. It's my first day.
Perhaps you'd care to stay and play?

THE WITCH'S ITCH

Which itch was it that itched the witch?
Which witch was it who itched?
Which witch was it who ditched the itch?
Which witch's itch was ditched?
Which ditched itch switched from itch to twitch?
Which witch now twitched instead of itched?
Which itch or twitch or witch would snitch?
I never knew quite which.

57

HORROR MOVIES

Hey, did you see the one
    where the girl's face is in stitches?

No. Did you see the one
    about those horrible witches?

Nope. How about the man with the ax?

Not me. Did you see "Monster Attacks?"

Missed it. How about the guy who
    was melted in wax?

Uh-uh. How about the one where
    he broke people's backs?

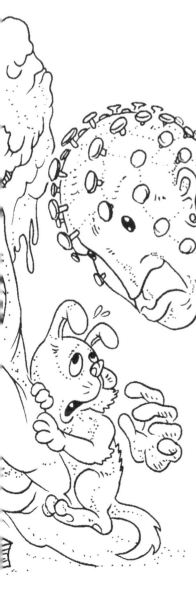

No way. How about the guy whose
    face had those tacks?

Not me.

You didn't? Neither did I!

I hate horror movies—
    I get scared and I cry!

Is that true?—Wow.
    Me too!!!!

'POSSUM

A 'possum is living under my bed!
I met him last night.
    He said his name's Fred.
Quite a nice fellow, and guess what he said?
"Bring me sardines and a little rye bread."

I brought him his food and we chatted a while.
He nibbled and dribbled,
        then started to smile.
He tiredly yawned and guess what he said?
"Would you sleep underneath because I'd like the bed?"

SIGH!
She threw me out!

61

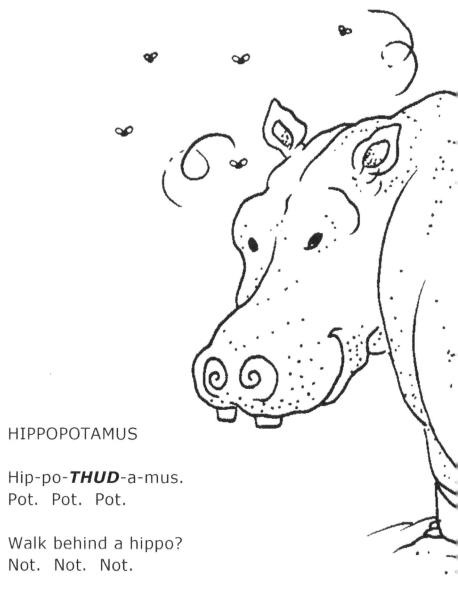

HIPPOPOTAMUS

Hip-po-**THUD**-a-mus.
Pot. Pot. Pot.

Walk behind a hippo?
Not. Not. Not.

Thud. Thud. Thud.
Caked cracked mud.

Hip-po-pot-a-**MUD**.
Thud. Thud. Thud.

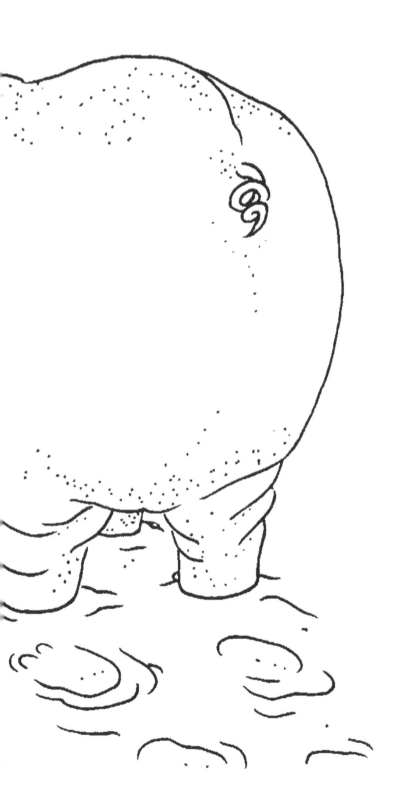

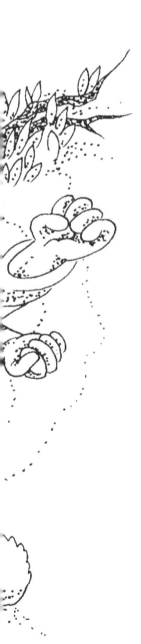

SOUNDS

Hear the blue bird at the tree?
Tap. Tap. Tap.

Hear my hand upon my knee?
Slap. Slap. Slap.

Hear the slippers on the floor?
Flap. Flap. Flap.

Hear my neighbor at the door?
Rap. Rap. Rap.

Hear the branches on the lawn?
Snap. Snap. Snap.

Hear me stretch my arms and yawn?
Nap. Nap. Nap.

WANNA BE

I wanna be the pitcher.
I wanna be the star.
I wanna be the batter,
hitting baseballs very far!

I wanna be the quarterback.
I wanna make the play.
I wanna score the touchdown.
I wanna save the day!

I wanna be the tagger.
I wanna be the "it."
I wanna run away and hide,
I don't wanna sit!

I wanna be the cowboy.
I don't wanna be the horse.
I wanna be the sheriff.
I'd be the best, of course!

I wanna be, I wanna be,
I wanna be it all,
I wanna be, please let me be...
I don't wanna be this small!

WELCOME TO THE BIG TENT

Welcome to the Big Tent.
Our fabulous show begins.
Hear Baby Brooklyn blowing raspberries.
Watch Debbie as she spins.
Caitlin walks the stairs in tights.
Gauge is our burping donkey.
Ryan twists his fingers back.
Araminta is a monkey.
Jenny hides behind a sheet
and never will come out.
Elyse will only whisper,
while Gabe will sing and shout.
Randy's tongue can touch his nose.
Mariah wags her ears.
Jordan turns his eyelids out.
Nicole cries crocodile tears.
Tyler twists his legs around
'til they're behind his head.
Cory is the best of all
pretending to be dead.
Kylie blows gigantic bubbles.
Kim's a barfing clown.
Gary wears his baggy pants.
Come watch them falling down.

Come one. Come all.
Now don't be slow.

Welcome to our wonderful show!

MY PERFECT ROW OF RACE CARS

I like my race cars lined up so.
Just leave them in a perfect row.
When I awake, I like to see—
them lined up right in front of me.

PEEKIN' 'ROUND THE CORNER

Peekin' 'round the corner,
> quiet as a mouse,
I hear people laughing,
> somewhere in the house.

Peekin' 'round the corner,
> fingers 'round the wall,
silently shuffle nearer,
> down and down the hall.

Peekin' 'round the corner,
> my pajamas slipping low,
a cold chill running up my spine,
> I just got to know.

Peekin' 'round the corner,
> my eyes squinting at their light,
who's visiting my parents
> in the middle of the night?

Peekin' 'round the corner,
> 'round and then around,
I can see the people,
> but now they've heard my sound.

Runnin' back 'round corners,
> no longer can I creep,
flip myself back into bed,
> and quick pretend to sleep.

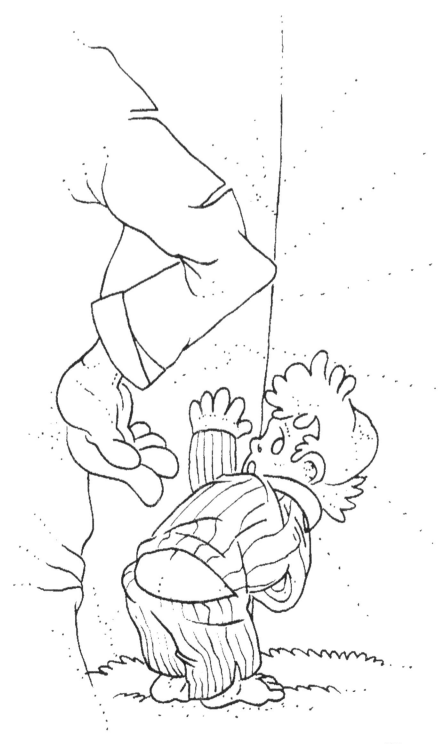

NIGHT-NIGHT

Upstairs. Downstairs. 'Round the hall and 'round.
Daffodils. Whipperwills. Summer is so blonde.
Ecru is the autumn. Winter's blanket's white.
Count all the stars in heaven. Time to say night-night.

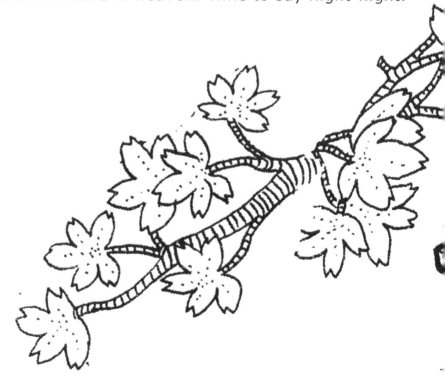

INDEX

A Child Only a Mother Could Love, 1
Answer These Questions, 42

Busybody Bumblebee, 39

Cousin Skylar's Got the Biggest Bite, 16

Dad and I Watch Sunday Football, 4

Fish (haiku), 38

Gertie McDougle, 20
Gwen the Hen, 18

Hippopotamus, 62
Horror Movies, 58
How to Build a Birdhouse, 2

I Am My Dad's Mechanic, 24
If..., 34
I Had a Horrible Nightmare Last Night, 32
Itches Inside My Head #1, 28
Itches Inside My Head #2, 52
I Told a Lie, 40

Loveable Lily, 6

Mini Menagerie Merry-Go-Round, 47
My Parents Tell Me I Can Be, 12
My Perfect Row of Race Cars, 70

Night-night, 74
Nothing Is Really That Strange, 31

Oh!, 26
Oops!, 8

Peekin' 'Round the Corner, 72
'Possum, 60

Shelby and Amour, 45
Sounds, 65

Tattoo!, 53
The Beastie Boy, 54
The Beauty Mark, 11
The Inside Out Inn at Outsville, 15
There's a Giant Sleeping Under My Bed, 22
The Morning Birds, 36
The Thrill, 51
The Witch's Itch, 56

Wanna Be, 66
Welcome to the Big Tent, 68
Wonderful Wanda, 48

AFTERWORD (WITH A BONUS POEM!)

There are so many poets and writers who inspire me and make me laugh, often until I cry and my sides begin to hurt.

These wordsmiths, these raconteurs and troubadours tug at my heart, make me reach for the sky, howl at the moon, trip over my tongue, cross my eyes, scratch my head, pull my ears, and when I was young, sometimes after reading their works to my parents, I'd get threatened to have my mouth washed out with soap.

These venerable fibbers, tall tale tellers, and conjurers enriched my life, changed my life, given me a new life and new perspectives on life, making me want to live life to its fullest and laugh all the way.

If you haven't met them, allow me to introduce you to a few of them: Eve Merriam, Dorothy Parker, Ogden Nash, Groucho Marx, Yogi Berra, Dr. Seuss, Billy Collins, e.e. cummings, Will Rogers, George Carlin, Jane Yolen, and the inimitable Shel Silverstein.

If you haven't read them, take one of their books out of the library, look them up online, or even purchase a few. Hopefully, you'll find that many of them will pull you in and speak to your heart.

I also want to introduce you to the two artists who have contributed to this book.

Luke Valentine's artwork is outstanding. Complex, subtle, engaging, humorous, shadowy, and at times seductively simple, he outrageously captures virtually all of the essence of the poems he illustrates.

Garrett Madlock recently joined the fun illustrating the dedication page and back cover. His work is light and airy, and more will be showcased in the second volume of this series. He is a very talented artist, and we are proud to have him onboard.

I would be remiss if I didn't acknowledge the wonderful support, hard work, and creative spirit of Heather Slawecki of graylynpress.com. She has been absolutely terrific, I adore her, and invite all of you who may need an editor, formatter, art designer, website creator/manager, and confidant to contact her at graylynpress.com. Thank you, Heather, so much!

And to my wife, Debbie, who has been my strength, my rock, and the love of my life. Thank you. What great times we've had raising our kids, along with all the "family meetings" on Monday nights, and tending to the chickens, ducks, horses, dogs, cats, birds, turtles, hamsters, koi, butterflies, and more. And thank you for your patience, encouragement, and help with this book and all my writings.

I end this Afterward with what is called a nonce poem.

A nonce is a one-time use poetic format in which I as the poet get to make up the rules for how to write in this particular style. I have named this particular nonce form, which you will read on the following page, a Calzone. It is a tribute to four of my favorite poets.

A Calzone, which you cannot know about because I'm making this up as we go along, is a complex, centuries-old Italian verse form that can have any number of lines, rhymed or not, in any meter, regular or irregular. But it must include references to three or more well-known poets. It must have a particular phrase beginning in the third line of the poem that is repeated throughout the poem. Lastly, a Calzone must pose a question that demands an answer though the answer may not ultimately be apparent to anyone—even by the end of the poem. Because it is a mystery, this style has continued for centuries (and none of this is true, hence, the word "nonce" as this is all a bunch of nonsense).

Now, if you would, please turn your attention to the following page.

The Discussion of Nonce at the Poetry Roundtable: A Calzone

So, what makes a poem nonce?
A student of Ogden Nash asked once.

That's exactly it, Nash said.
The student stared and scratched his head.

Shel Silverstein rose up from his chair,
adding, *I see nonce everywhere,*

to Nash's, *That's exactly it.*
Dorothy Parker chimed in, *Kismet.*

Truly, Nash lovingly responded to her wit
and once again exclaimed, *That's exactly it!*

Eve Merriam bellowed, *How insightful,*
but I believe all your explanations are frightful.

What makes a poem nonce,
none of you have answered once.

That's exactly it! Nash said.
Eve replied, *Nash. You're quite the knucklehead!*

The answer to: What is nonce?
she shrugged and said, *Not once.*

Then it's twice, Nash replied. *That's exactly it!*
And that was all the discussion that he would permit.

Originally published in The Reach of Song 2021, The Georgia Poetry Society, Atlanta, Georgia.

ABOUT THE AUTHOR

Randy Mazie has a Master of Science in Social Work (MSSW) from Columbia University and a Master of Business Administration (MBA) from Barry University.

He worked for a decade with the New York State Office of Mental Health and other social agencies as well as for over thirty years with Miami-Dade County Public Schools.

He has had numerous nonfiction articles published in professional journals, and fiction pieces, short stories as well as poetry, published in such journals as Defenestration, The MacGuffin, DASH, Light, The Gyroscope Review, The Orchards Poetry Journal, YourDailyPoem.Com, the Anthology of Transcendent Poetry, Cosmographia Books, 2019, and The Reach of Song Anthology, Georgia Poetry Society, 2021, among other journals and books.

This is his first book in a series titled ITCHES INSIDE MY HEAD.

Mr. Mazie can be contacted at:
mail@ayearofencouragements.com.